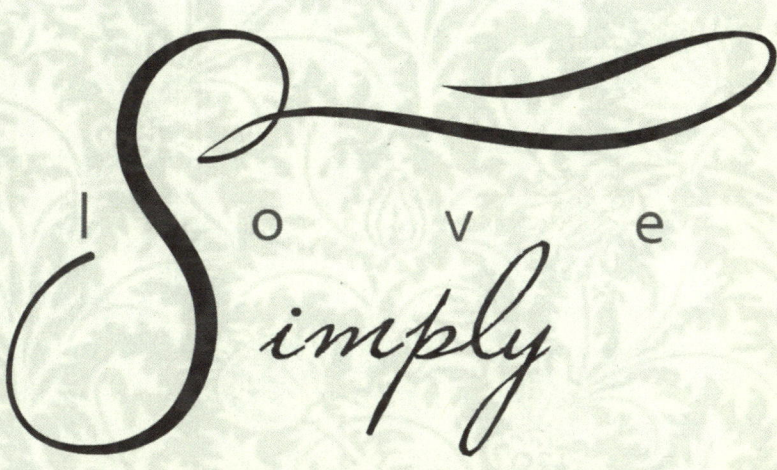

simply sherri

Love Simply
By Simply Sherri
© 2015

ISBN 978-1-387-47853-8

Introduction

— F. Scott Fitzgerald once said:

"Writers aren't people exactly. Or, if they're any good, they're a whole lot of people trying so hard to be one person."

I'm a
Lady
Writer
Crazy
Lover
Sexy
I never lose my cool
These are the adjectives some use to describe my personality
In these pages, you will meet each different incarnation

Spectrum	6
Thought Process (Senyru)	8
Timeline	9
Quiet Confidence	11
Forty-Five	14
Timeline Part 2	16
Senryū ~ Knights	18
Competition	19
Sixty-Nine	21
That Red Dress	23
Sherri Had A Little Man	25
Senryū ~ Forever	27
Poetry And Jazz	28
Epilogue	29
Liquefy	30
Senyru ~ Waterfal	32
Kiss Me	33
I Fell	35
Something	36
Kryptonite	37
Naked	38
Free Agency	40
Intertwined	42
Chapters	43
Don't Know…We Are	44
Morning After	46
They Taught Me	47
Destructive Beauty	50
Sparkly Things	51
Half-Staff	54
Window	56
Translations	58
That Moment	60
To The Man At Rite Aid	61
Cracked	63
Split Second	65
Poison	67
A Little Bit…	69
Superman	71

Love Letters	73
Three Generations	77
Family Tree	78
He Calls Me	79
Works Cited	81

Spectrum

She often dressed in a royal hue
Luxurious, creative, with the wonder of a child
In lilac to eggplant
She strides through life…

He dreams of her in crimson
Immediacy, fire, devilish
Or rose tones
Tender, sensitive and sexual
The spectrum's love tints

In person, he dresses her in aureolin
Energetic, optimistic, warm
No romance in the aura
Just confusion
The pigments blend
Creating amber or low flame….
Attraction, stimulating close enough to happiness
It's accepted as love
Lived like great romance
Missing some of the passion

Her inner fire is hard to maintain
when only half-tended; the royal—
Over time it fades
Leaving indigo
Cooler, lonelier than before the merger
Yet she remains calm through the storms

Never searching for the trees, they still discover forest
Envy, jealously
Natural feelings when embracing lust
Calling it love
Encased in a half-truth
They become blinded
Struggle to maintain their status
Start being aggressive

The image diminishes into ebony
Absence of everything; no meaning
They injure each other while
Killing the pseudo relationship

they should have stayed in sunshine
instead of nearing the fire
ending up

burned

Thought Process (Senyru)

Negative questions
Stunt growth opportunities
Be optimistic

Timeline

1 minute from now
We will be Walking hand in and out of these doors
Smiling and giggling as we get started on

2 hours from now
Heading out of town on getaway
taking time from our grind and stress

3 days from now
Create our own definition of dreamland
Under the light of the full moon on beach of black sand

4 weeks from now
Our impulsive moment of ecstasy
Has planted a slow growing seed

5 months from now
Preparing our new home for the addition to our nest
I never knew that we could be this blessed

When

5 months ago
You laid out your vision for our future
 Assuring me that my forever is safe & secure

4 weeks ago
Making simple plans, getting anxious
Asking our closest friends to meet us

3 days ago
We Could get our paperwork from the justice
Fulfilling your earlier Promise

2 hours ago
Arriving at our pastor's office to take our vows
All our dreams are coming true now

1 minute ago
Elated and ready to cry
he said "Groom you may kiss your bride"

Quiet Confidence

It must be hard work being ratchet
Running through life
Acting like home training
Lessons were taught but never to be practiced
Showing their ass at every opportunity
Always bringing drama
For a purpose, yet to be determined
To feel important
To gather attention
Expending massive amounts of time and energy
Thinking of new ways to shock and amaze the masses
Attempting to impress an audience
That no longer finds them entertaining
People don't care enough to know who to call for them
in case of emergency

These women are happy to exist in the belief that
Well-behaved women seldom make history
Condoleezza Rice, Indira Gandhi, Madame Curie, Maya Angelou
Didn't contribute much to society, did they,
While still being ladies

Don't get me wrong even proper women act up occasionally
Susan B Anthony, Malala Yousafzai, Rosa Parks
For a moment in time
They put their good manners aside for a greater purpose
They are known for the results of the work
Not just the actions they took

I've seen the pictures
Simpler times
Ladies would put on their finest attire
Dressed to be seen
Just to walk down the street
Having pleasant conversations with whomever they meet

Women today dress their best
To make a scene
Head to an event just to start a fight

For some petty reason
Modeling their actions after something
They saw in scripted reality TV

Remember
Those women get paid to always be on
their most bankrupt behavior
Supporting their broke and fabulous lifestyles
embarrassing their mothers,
Their ancestors
Thankfully it only takes two clicks to change the channel
Their table flipping shouting matches no longer in my existence
I wish it was that easy in real life
Differentiating the sane from the crazy is becoming difficult
What will our descendants think of the evidence we leave behind?
Twerk videos, pornos and pictures
 with middle fingers proudly displayed
Will they think
A simpler time or that's when women became the punch line
We were once considered queens
Quick to correct anyone who called us out our names
Today bitch is a term for the one in the mirror
Will call their best friend a whore to her face
Yet demand respect from strangers
When they have made a joke of themselves

Embarrassing their mothers, the ancestors
By extension me
Regardless of my nature and personality
I'm judged always to be angry
Too weak because I refuse to attend
Any shouting match I'm invited too
I refuse to engage
The one who believes talking cruder and louder
Equals intelligence

Real gangsters move in silence not violence
I accomplish more with a smile, a nod and a glance
They don't understand how much strength it takes
As she is acting crazy
To look a woman in the face
Turn around and walk away
Real bad girls are the silent type
That's why they don't understand why
They are slowly dying inside around me
Quiet confidence kills them every time

Forty-Five

You are never to ask a woman her age
I'm excited to say I turned 45 today
Not saying every day was perfect
I claim all my mistakes
I've also learned a few lessons along the way

Be mindful of the pieces that keep your mind peaceful
Separating self from your personal obsessions
is the key ingredient to the recipe for avoiding the
 descent into madness
Lesson learned: live passionately

There are people paid to pass judgment
God has the final say on how I lived my life
So "don't judge me" no longer exists in my vocabulary
Lesson learned: live fully

I've seen some dark days
Attended funerals of too many friends and classmates
My heart broke the day I was told
A heart attack put my high school sweetheart in a cemetery;
 he was 36
Lesson learned: live for those that can't; stop existing…

Love and lose, love and lose but keeping trying
Don't 'hate' Love
Can't find it if you give up on it
Each go round in the relationship wars
is one step closer to the one
Lesson Learned: live and love often

The common thread is to live
I'm excited to start this next chapter of my life
Outside the lines
No rule book
Unscripted…
My friends would say do it like I'm doing it for color TV

I can't
They will need a screen much bigger and glasses that are 3D
Because I'm going to do it big
I have no clue what is about to happen to me
But I ask you to join me
Or if you can't I'll find you some glasses
so you can watch…

Timeline part 2

5 months ago
I met a man that took my heart
I wish I knew a change was coming
before

4 weeks ago
You morphed into a man I barely knew
should have been my clue
when

3 days ago
you called said we needed to talk
I should have suspected
you were about to walk

2 hours ago
Out of the door and out of my life
thought we were destined to walk the aisle
finally

1 minute ago
The tears stopped flowing
I guess I should be happy to be

Free so

1 minute from now
I'll get up off this floor,
compose myself
take off this ring

2 hours from now
I'll start praying for peace
understanding
ability to forgive him

3 days from now
I will be able to take a breath
not think about the dream now dead

4 weeks from now
I will recognize myself as a single
My life will restart.

5   months from now
When I have learned from my mistakes
A new man will have the opportunity
to open my heart.

Senryū ~ Knights

Chivalry death ruled
Voluntary manslaughter
A strong woman charged

Competition

Self-worth should not be determined by any decision made at 5 o'clock in the morning
Or too much past 6pm
Yet there they stand, the last two women in full game face
One black
One red
Playing a child's game during a chess match
With no queen the board
The prize: one stand with this modern day knight
He has no castle keys, no honor and no loyalty
Just a pretty smile, a hard dick and not promising anything
Still they are ready to take their place
with the nameless and faceless
Who have played in this tournament before
Both lack the understanding that by starting this competition
They both have already lost
For this man is choosing
And he doesn't have too
He is just waiting for one to decide she's tired
of simple maneuvering
Pick up her pride chips and go home
No effort, no chase no mystery
There is barely chemistry
Yet the both stand strong playing
Thinking it's gonna be me

It's now 5:30

Still waiting
Still playing
Still

Each is more prepared to take his penis into her hands
instead of her own destiny
Ready to use all her all her gifts and tricks to make him ready
For the sex he kinda sorta wants
With a woman he will soon forget
An act that will be flushed away moments after it's over
Yet each believes she is one move closer to the crown and throne

That has never been proffered nor shown
Had each valued herself more than the prize desired
They would have been long gone
Yes home alone
But with their dignity intact
The shames in their walks need not to exist
There is more beauty and grace in the forfeit

What did that girl say in that movie?
Sometimes when you win, you really lose,
Sometimes when you lose, you really win,
And if you win or lose you actually tie (Shelton, 1992)

He is just tying the knot at the end of her rope to
 keep them hanging on
They're still making simple moves, just jumping

It's now 6am

He's had no interaction with the childish contest
going on before him
For he's too drunk and too tired to care
Acutely aware that if push came to shove
He could handle the release himself

The game seems to be winding down
I'm ready to hit the timer
I'll let you pick the winner
Is it the one who took the L as she ascended the stairs
Or she who surrendered the king as she walked out the door

Sixty-Nine

I'm taking the risk talking about this
Another woman may take this poem as a blueprint
To try and separate me from mine
But it's a chance I'll take

He likes sixty-nine

I knew this going in
We discussed it
Handling this situation like adults
We put all our desires on the table
There'd be no questions later
He said he'd like our heads to often meet
Our energy is best exchanged that way
We balance each other like yin and yang
I excel at taking him all in
He's an expert at keeping me engaged in the act
So he keeps coming back…
To 69:

Everything he wants from me is 69 inches off the floor
He likes how I give brain
Or shall I say, he likes how I use my head
How I filled it with information
How I have my own opinions is what keeps him intrigued
That I shoot straight from the hip with
 rhyme, wisdom and whimsy
That he is so impressed by what this does
That he almost forgets what the rest of me does
How he uses his extended inches around my 36 inches
Is completely secondary
I have never cut me in half
Or been treated me like a collection of human sex toys
He enjoys me whole

Even though tongue lips fingers have explored, touch
 and tasted every inch
What keeps that
Crooked smile on his face is this:
My head game is vicious

I was in his head before I was on it, and
I'll still be there long after I'm gone

And though we are far past the time when
we will continue to grow
Anyone can get on my level by using your head a little better...

That Red Dress

Standing in front of my wardrobe
Contemplating my day's uniform
That red dress
Taunted me like a
Mischievous nymph
Having hibernated throughout the winter
Patiently waiting for any day's warm weather
Even though yesterday's temps were a tease
Quietly, she called, "Release me"
Shaking my head; am I hearing things?
The words come again
"Release me"
At first surprised
Now hypnotized
I'm only able to obey the dress's command

Apparently, that red dress had a plan

It picked that new matching set from Frederick's
Caused me to paint my face and color my lips
Made sure my scent was flowery and
My locs were flowing freely
Then that nymph wandered through my pumps
Found the pair she wanted still in the box:
Black patent leather peep toe stilettos—
She wanted to show off the pedicure

Before we make our exit
We check our reflection
Pleased with what
What she sees
I grab my purse and keys
Me and the dress leave
On the streets passing men of many nationalities
In their native tongues' I hear them speak
Aahh bonita (Spanish)
Sie ist schön (German)
Elle est belle (French)
Ela é linda (Portuguese)

All saying the same thing:
"DAMN, she's beautiful!"

However, this praise is not what she wanted
So quickly away from work I sauntered
My actions still controlled by the red dress
I guess she really knew what was best
We made a call to my baby
"Lunch outside your company"
His response was an eager, "Yes, baby; please"
I still didn't know what the nymph had in mind
However, I got a clue when at my man's office I arrived
Heard him channel Johnny Gill in a sigh: "My, my, my"
Then that nymph really started to work her voodoo
With the look in his eye we both knew
Eating was not on the menu
Quickly we found a private place
Swiftly we made space
Hastily lifted the dress
Positioned my legs
As the dress begged
Roughly he pushed the thong aside
Then
Suddenly he was inside
Thrusting aggressively
You would have thought
This would be his last piece
He had me screaming for mercy
That orgasm
Was cataclysmic
Damn that was some good shit
How did we get here?
What transpired?
I guess that nymph got what she required
After I released
The hypnosis ceased
My baby gave me a kiss on the cheek
And I was free to leave
The nymph is back asleep
Now I know why HE bought me that dress
He knew about that crazy nymph that was in it

Sherri had a little man

Sherri had a little man

Not in stature
I like them big and tall
It was his thinking that was small
He was unoriginal

Sherri had a little man
He thought of her often this we know

He spent too much thinking about hitting it from behind
Practicing lame pickup lines
What's your name, what's your sign
Instead of just starting with HELLO
My name is…

Sherri had a little man
He thought of her often this I know
Everywhere Sherri's conversation went

His game is tailored to women who are more basic
Her mind flows from the sublime to the ridiculous.
He's not sure what to do
He's just dazed and confused

Sherri had a little man
He thought of her often this we know
Everywhere Sherri's conversation went
This man couldn't follow

He thought conversation unnecessary
Stopping his part with a smile and a wink
The women he wooed before were shallow
There was no need for him to think…

Sherri had a little man
He thought of her often this we know
Everywhere Sherri's conversation went
This man couldn't follow

He followed her around a poetry show one day

Unprepared to come out of the cold
Happy to lurk in the shadows
Stalking and staring
Plotting and doing nothing

Sherri had a little man
He thought of her often this we know
Everywhere Sherri's conversation went
This man couldn't follow
He followed her around the poetry show one day
He made no action; Sherri ignored him
Him not acting is against the rules

Anything worth having
Is more than worth the effort
Whether or not she thinks you are attractive
Or if she's already decided I want to do that
You my friend still have to talk yourself into it

So, little man…

Your inaction speaks volumes
I need you to lean in start the game
Make your best play
The woman that may change your life
Is ONE "HELLO" AWAY

Senryū ~ Forever

Yesterday we struggled
Today cherish moments
Tomorrow… destined

Poetry and Jazz

No audience
No microphone stand
No stage
Just a dimly lit venue…
Me and you
Face to face
Toe to toe
No words spoken
There is poetry going on
Our verses exchanged telepathically
Message delivered clearly
Clear like Kirk Whalum's saxophone
On a jazz tune
I wanna know
How we stay in this place
Stay in this melody
Melding jazz and my words
Into a song everybody sings
While standing silently

Epilogue

I know I am not supposed to
Judge a book by its cover
But as soon as I saw you
I wanted to move straight to the epilogue
Listen to the voice of our descendant
Reminisce about our love affair
Pass over the drama, plot twists and missteps
Forget discovering the protagonist and the antagonist
Just skip to the part where we are living happily ever after
I will be more than happy give you a synopsis
The prologue:
My life before this moment

Chapter 1:
       Our chance meeting at this park

Chapter 2:
       Early dates without the cat and mouse games

Chapter 3:
       first time we make love with our clothes on

Chapter 4 – 13:
  Describes our lives

       Relationship
        Wedding
         Children

Do you want more of the book review?
Or can I say "Hello…"
Start to live all those tomorrows
Loving our way to the epilogue…

Liquefy

It was an ordinary crisp Indian Summer Day
The sinking sun shined on two sitting in the park
Talking
Intermittently
Him laughing
Her giggling

The casual observers would wonder
What was the topic of their conversation that had them so absorbed in each other?
For they had not broken the gaze for a moment
The two of them involved recognize it was the most important conversation
About everything and nothing
Exploiting the time enjoying each other's company
Just…being

Without warning the mystical happened
It was the simplest of motions most wouldn't notice
Though it only took mere seconds
To me it occurred in slow motion

He brushed a hair away from my face

When the back of his hand touched my forehead
His energy jolted through me like lightening
As his palm passed my peripheral
The upturn of his lips inferred he could read my thoughts
As his finger continued to trace my cheek
A vision of our future was implanted into my psyche
When his thumb skimmed my chin
Instantaneously I knew he was my destiny.

All the glaciers of doubt that surrounded my heart
Melted
All the pools of fear in my head…
Evaporated
All the clouds of insecurity in my spirit
Vanished
I fell in love in just one motion
There should be a law against
This moment so intimate happening in public
With everyone watching we made love
In one motion that took less than five seconds

Sitting on parking bench
On a crisp Indian Summer day

Senyru ~ Waterfal

As each droplet falls
From the lake behind my eyes
Liberates my soul

Kiss Me

Kiss me...

Leave me a quivering mass of anticipation
Of what comes next
Let sunlight drenched dreams
Be replays of that moment
Our lips last connected...

Keep
It
Sweet
Sustained

Ignore our surroundings
Who may be watching
Engage a kiss that changes everything
Make it Oscar worthy
From here to eternity
Imprint your lips in my soul's cement
Make their impression on my heart permanent

Keep
Intentional
Strong
Steady

With intention
With New Year's Eve expectations that
Yes, tomorrow we start a new
Kiss me
Until you taste the dry grapes
Get drunk in love off Sherri
You're stumbling

Lace your lips with

Love
Sensuality
Devotion
LSD

Make me see hallucinations

Kaleidoscope
Images
Stars
Spiraling

Let me stay HIGH…
Soar with the angels

Kill
Insecurities'
Silent
Shadow and
Slay my fears

Let my lips graze your Adam's apple
They can die here

Kiss me
Frequently
Until it becomes unnatural not too

I Fell

I fell in love with how neatly our puzzle pieces fit. We are complete as individuals but more beautiful together
I fell in love with the merriment in your eyes when mischief is afoot
I feel in love with your spirit and how easily you lift mine
I fell in love with the sensation of our fingers intertwined and you squeeze gently
I fell in love with how we complete each other's thoughts silently
I fell in love with the strength you exude standing stoically, observing
I fell in love with how you watch over me
I fell in love with you differently each time we met. It felt like the first time… Every time
I fell in love with the pictures of our future you painted
I fell in love with you completely and can't wait to find you… ONE day

Something

We are going to be something
More than friends
Less than committed
And I will feel all those special warm and fuzzies throughout it
Engaged in every conversation
Process each bit of information
Extend that pause between attraction and intimacy
I believe this is what they call DATING…

I've seen this chemistry added a short fuse and sparked it before
Fireworks while beautiful; when misfired they hurt
So why don't we let it slow burn for a bit…
Allow my sweet and your salt mix to really infuse
Take the time, make the effort to make it wonderful

Kryptonite

He placed it in my hand
No warning labels
without instructions
Just his faith in his eyes
That I'd do no harm
The energy palpable
Power barely containable
When I looked down
The rainbow escaping
Through my fingers
Frightening
He told me don't worry
Recounted the following story
I can only give this to someone I trust
The ability to impair me
Green weakens momentarily
Red incapacitates permanently
Blue rebuilds me
Gold destroys me
(Now I'm really nervous)
He continues
See why this gift is so precious
I give to you my angel
The power to make me mortal
The capacity to turn Superman
To Clark Kent
My darling please protect it
My Achilles heel, my personal
Form of Kryptonite

Tonight, my baby

I give you…

My heart

Naked

Can I undress in front of you?
be so naked with you
that all my scars, flaws
and imperfections
are in full view…
without doubting your love for me
is
true

Can I speak of my fears?
Shed a few tears
Drop my luggage
They are getting too heavy
For me to carry
However
I am afraid to unpack.
I am not ready to face
The demons that are inside
I have been folding, unfolding
Adjusting, repackaging, redistributing
And adding
And adding
And adding
More weight
That I am no longer sure
The stories, drama, hurt, pain
They contain
They are just a part of me

I cannot just release
What I need is an exorcism
To remove my demons
I need to escape from the 5th level
Of the Inferno, I was sent to
In order to reach Paradise with you

Will you hold my hand?
Guide me up through each circle
Through the beast of purgatory
To the plateau where the warmth
Of the sun shines forever on our shoulders

So I ask again…
Can I undress in front of you?
Be so naked with you
That all my scars, flaws
And imperfections
Are in full view…
Without doubting your love for me
Is
True

Free Agency

He said he's tired of saying goodnight to me in text messages
Our friendship has gone beyond that
This last communication of the day
Should be up close...personal...
Murmured between sheets and kisses
Awakened
With hushed morning greetings
Sweet sweet nothings
Cheshire cat smiles
Legs entangled
Skin melded together
Are there really two of us here
His arms have us locked
In this position ...
His fingers interlaced in my locs
My fingers caressing the back of neck
Decisions need to be made
Sleep or go again ...
Decisions, decisions
Before protests start
Hair is pulled
Neck exposed
Soft kisses from chin to breast bone
groan
Yes ... that dream is exquisite
Two people in the midst of lovemaking
But ummmm
We just wanted to fuck ...
Release the pent up energy
Engage in some acts having us
Unable to look each other in the eye
Or at least not with a straight face
Let our bodies and hormones have the conversation
Our hearts need not participate in...

We've come too far down this I actually kind of like you road
For the sport fucking ...
We've become professionals at
Undrafted free agents

Switching teams just by switching hats
We know how to do that…
no franchise tags
giving just enough to keep our status on someone's
active on the roster for next week
We see each other differently …
No blinders
We actually see each other….
No filters,
Or rose colored glasses clouding our view

The desire for more of a connection
Has us studying the playbooks
Which kiss quickens my breathing
Which lick arches by back
Which suck gets that leg to vibrate
Which touches causes my eyes to roll back

Since I'm nonverbal
He's trying to figure out
the combination to get me to scream
where that spot is that causes me to buck to hard
I throw him off
literally
I can get him to let go
Control his freak for a minute
Can he stay in my rhythm
As I'm drawing life out of him
Cause him to speak in tongues
YES

It's going to be that good
We want it to stay that way
Retire from the game
Forever

So until we are ready for all of it …
It's best we stay away from each other

Intertwined

Gazing into coffee colored eyes

I wonder

Would I
Could I
Should I…

Delve into your dreams to extract
The picture of you and I
Intertwined
Engaged in a kiss
Tangled tongues
Knitted limbs
Passion's fire blazing
Bathed in cool moonlight

I reflect
I sigh
I smile

At the fantasy-filled image
Defying reality

We are
Closer than eyes can perceive
Affection existing deeper than an ocean's abyss
Union forged through time's trials and tribulations
Connections fused at nerve endings

Our thoughts
Our hearts
My fate
Your destiny
Collide and combine

Spiritually
Individually
We die
Reincarnated as one soul
Always Intertwined

Chapters

My girlfriends asked me if my new man was cute
I have no idea…
Yes, I can pick my man out of a line up
I just have no idea if he is attractive or not
Whether or not his appearance is pleasing to the masses
The cover has never mattered
I was three chapters into his book
When I realized I was reading
And I didn't want to put the book down
Wrapped in his pages
Immersed in the story
Holding fast through the scary parts
Engaged in the experience that is him

I've had to force my eyes to focus
Pressure the retina to interface with the optic nerve
to connect to the part of the brain
that determines whether or not he has sex appeal

Does it really matter?
When his voice is like music
Soothes the savage beast in me
Laying on his chest
Free Stress reliever
Falling asleep next to him
Better than any sedative

So no it wasn't love at first site
I'm still not sure I've ever really seen him
I've just read his chapters and now I'm excited to write our own

Don't Know...We Are

Cacao seeds don't know they are sweet
Planted, grown, roasted then mixed into a confection
Craved, desired, deemed essential to the masses

Hearts don't know the uniqueness of their rhythm
They just start beating
Keeping pace regardless of circumstance

Roses don't know they're beautiful
They just grow on sidewalks and hillsides
Rainbow painting the landscape wherever they exist

Diamonds don't know their brilliance
Formed over time with pressure to be multifaceted
It takes an expert to determine their value

These are the things symbolizing affection
Sweet
Rhythm
Beautiful
Brilliance

Women, we are sweet
Grown and mixed with experiences
Craved, desired, deemed essential to the masses

Women have a uniqueness in our rhythm
We just keep breathing, keep stepping
Keeping pace regardless of circumstance

Women are beautiful
We flourish in city streets and countryside
Rainbow painting the landscape wherever we exist

Women are brilliant
Formed over time with pressure to be multifaceted
It takes an expert to determine our true value

We are love in action in action

Remember that

Morning After

Apparition
Hallucination
Figment of my imagination
Possibly it was just a dream
Slowly turning into a living nightmare
Here one minute gone the next
Blemishes unnoticeable to the naked eye
Nothing to examine to provide proof
Leaving zero evidence, its existence questioned

Articles claimed
Pillows unscented
Absent remnants

Physically searching would be time wasted
Only witness left speechless in aftermath
Love Scene Investigators would be baffled
Hundreds of questions are left unanswered
In corners of mind visions appear
Dream or nightmare, fantasy or reality

Vivid memory
Make believe
Fairy tale

They Taught Me

Gentlemen
Watch how you treat a woman
Statistically she will outlive you
Given several more years to tell my version of the story
depending on the type of woman the story might
skew the report perfectly to make sure that she's always the wronged party
Or poems and essays can be written about love
Masters Level College classes are dedicated to the great love stories
Elizabeth Barrett Browning and Emily Dickenson
will still be dissected 100 years from today
Watch how you treat the women make sure you control how our story is reported
someday a woman will say…

I don't know what happen between you and my mother, she has never spoke of the full story, all I know is you two tried and tried and it didn't work. You will never know exactly how your absence has affected me but I know without you I do not exist. So for this you deserve thanks.
After all these years it takes more strength then either of us possess to try to make something of the tattered father daughter relationship. I appreciate the fact you keep trying. I'll do better.

The most disrespectful thing I do every day of my life is look this one man in his eye and call him by his first name, he's the one that chose to be my Dad. In my life since I was 5, marrying my mom when I was 6, in my corner fixing any problem, so anyone having issues with the fact I'm spoiled address it to him.

How will you be footnoted in my story…

You stole something from me, in such a way I know where it happens but something that can never be given back, taken by someone who called himself friend and confidant. I may have learned how to be stronger woman functioning with that nightmare replaying in my brain, only reason you are forgiven is because I needed to give the gift to myself. Your name will not be spoken by me again in this lifetime.

Think about how you would be scripted in the flashback scene:

Our first hello was over 30 years ago, we were kids then ... barely a year or two into adulthood when we finally found our way to couple-hood, my mother still compares every man I bring home to you. An officer and a gentleman, you always put us up where we belong we were just not mature enough to carry on. Often thought we'd find our way back to each other, fate had other plans. I hope your eternal rest will always be peaceful know I always think of you and smile.

You taught me that putting a ring on it doesn't guarantee a damn thing, but pretty pictures of me in ta big white dress ... it does mean security, guarantee happiness or together for eternity. Thank you for giving me my girls and my perspective on life, love and relationships and how not to make that mistake so easily again

Will your name change a definition in her life?

"Big brother," you taught me the meaning of persistence with a story has nothing to do with you
You gave me more family that defined "gentleman," "brotherhood," "cherishing"

The two of you with the same name: If you ever hear this you know why you are on this list, you two exist in all my erotic poems. Thank you and thank you.

Too many to name and number but you all represent naked intelligence always on display—refreshing to a woman who demands a high level of conversation. Thank you for being in this community with me.

Were you a speed bump on my way to something greater, a face and a name I no longer remember?

Are you a key player in biography of her life?

He discovered the poet behind the smile, planted the seed that is still reaping beauty. He provided a safe place for her to grow. To both of you I'm more than grateful.

I didn't know what the Arabic word for friend was…You have been so to me for more than a decade. Through every hurricane you have stood right by me, the eye in every storm. We are almost birth twins, will always be twin souls, regardless of who we eventually settle down with we are together forever.

We were in pieces when we met; we've created beautiful picture of friendship—a bond. Most will never understand how family is created by a simple "hello."

Untraditional, unexpected but the embodiment of Prince Charming; even though happily ever after isn't how our fairy tale ended, I still see the time we were together as a blessing. I hope to find someone else again.

To the one who came after, showing me how good it can be when all the puzzle pieces fit perfectly: I learned from you never to settle for less the next time.

Thank you all for all each of you has taught me; I'm ready now to live the lessons.

So when my search begins again and I meet the one and he starts plucking on my heart strings, I'll know my search for forever will be done.

Destructive Beauty

Sometimes beauty can only come after destruction
A rearrangement of the landscape is sometimes necessary
It changes the view
Causes us to rebuild
More often than not in the same place
Wildfires destroys everything in their path
As they creep across the terrain
Teasing the edges of the foundation
Coming close then moving away
We try to impede its progress
Efforts fruitless until the rains come
When the tears fall
we release the things haunting us
Failed relationship
Unrequited love
Unmet expectations
Deferred dreams
I've sent them up in flames
The tears fall
The ashes rise
With a phoenix
Wings spread wide
Surveying the new setting
What was lost in the fire?
Everything
That no longer needed
To soar…

Sparkly Things

I only say I love you when we're arguing
It's an abbreviation for
Yes, I'm still willing to put up with your bullshit
He responds similarly
As a reminder that there are a thousand reasons why I do
Even though in that moment I can't think of one of them
Later when it's all over I won't say I love you at all
It's not that I don't feel it when we are at peace
Or that my heart doesn't swell because of it
It's just the eight letters that make up those three little words
Are not big enough to contain what I feel for him
Saying I love you seems small
Recalling the reasons why I'm willing to climb these mountains
Traverse the peaks and valleys
Risk mind, body, soul and sanity…
There is only one reason:
It's in how he loves me

His love is a verb not a noun
His love is in practice not in things
It's always on display, unveiled to outsiders
Each and every one of his actions embody
I'm special to him…
It's written in his body language
Sealed inside every kiss

He empowers me
He makes better
He strengthens me
He inspires me

The relationship I always wanted
The type of love that exists
Without rings, without vows and without an officiant
I can do this without the extra paperwork
Commitment required; marriage optional

My view shaped by watching loving couples
Smiling, walking arm in arm…just doing

Or maybe it's my age and experience, or the fact that
I've already taken one marital
Step—
Make that, misstep—
Has me thinking being called "wife" again
May not be part of my construct

But don't get me wrong
The little girl in me would love to have the fantasy
Him down one knee presenting a ring
Because I like sparkly things
But all that glitters
Should not be

Cherished
As
Rare
Antique
Treasure

Give me

Consistency
Acceptance
Respect
Affection
Tenderness
Sincerity

Yea that's how I want my two carats
In a ring around our hearts for an infinity

Yes, diamonds are beautiful
And can cost thousands
But they have yet to cut the stone
To match the clarity of his eyes
The brilliance of his smile just when he looks at me
It's like every time he's never seen me that way
That look—that twinkle—is priceless
And my response

It's written all over your face
You don't have to say a word
Just smile a smile a smile
A smile for me
It's better than any word I ever heard [Rude Boys]

That sparkle…is pure, flawless…
And I'm not saying he is
Or this relationship is
But we live by our own definition
Making this work for us
It's natural
Beautiful
So, untraditional as it sounds, I will continue my boycott of peacefully whispering I love you

If he wants to hear how deeply I feel for him
We can sway wrapped in each other arms
I'll whisper in his ear:

You are my latest, my greatest inspiration
Keep lifting me up…
Higher and higher
Because
You inspire me

Half-Staff

The morning news opens with a picture of The White House
Silhouetted against the clear azure sky with the American flag flying at half staff
A symbol of respect that has lost some of its meaning
When it's that position for the fourth time in less than a year….
Flying in the low posture to honor the civilian casualties outside of any active war zone
12 more victims of yet another mass shooting

For too long
It was happening out there
Now it's happening right here
The body count keeps rising
We keep asking what can be done….
Looking over the capitol dome
They are flying the flag half-staff

I live in fear …
I can't
Send my babies to school
Send my young adult to campus
Can't go to the mall
Can't go to the movies
I can't go to church
Hell, I'm not safe on a secure military facility for the second time now

I haven't been able to go to work for years without fear of someone who has been pushed too far beyond their limits…too gone to know how to properly release the pressure, not sure how to handle their anger
So I'm left to find shelter in places, praying each day I make it home
Over the Supreme Court
They fly the flag half-staff

The "They" with the capital T will say it's just mental health issues to blame,
Too many desensitized by the violence in video games or some other excuse
He was a loner and we didn't know what he was planning
But the past few days he was acting kinda strange…
We didn't know how to help him …
Or don't care enough to try

Lobbyist espousing it's our right to bear arms
Tougher rules and background check violates our rights
I'm asking do we really need access to military grade weapons
Why is there a need for an assault rifles for hunting ducks and deer in open fields?
Well aware that the only prey being killed are humans in confined spaces
When all the pointing fingers and shouting is over
After the politicians have finished giving the lip services
What will we have...

Another candlelight vigil
Another moment of silence
And the government doing everything they can agree to do to prevent this from happening again

They will fly the flag at half-staff

Window

> *It's a beautiful day in this neighborhood,*
> *A beautiful day for a neighbor.*

…A beautiful day to walk past his window
Where he's in clear view of everybody
Almost naked
Almost naked
Only a small towel hiding his
Currently limp manhood
I only caught a fleeting glimpse
As I headed out to my car for church
I know today I'll have to repent
Maybe I can get a pass from my deacon
These sinful thoughts that are creeping
Are really not my responsibility
I didn't ask him to stand there
Parading his assets
Large Chest
Molded Arms
Sculpted Abs
If he'd turn around I could see the curve of his ass
Then I'd be left wondering
How high it goes when he is in mid stroke
Asking myself does he moan, or talk when he's hitting it
Even though outside its warm
My feet are froze
In this spot
Thinking would it be rude to walk up to his door
Knock quietly
Say a pleasant hello
Ask for some coffee
Invite him to come with me to church
Learn more about God in our worship

The view I saw is all what I want
We could do it missionary but the tile might be cold
Me on top riding rodeo in the dining room
I should get in my car and go

> *I have always wanted to have a neighbor just like you,*
> *I've always wanted to live in a neighborhood with you.*

Now I'm sitting my car
Sweating off my makeup
Banging my head into the steering column
I should be halfway to where I'm going
But here I still sit dreaming
That glimpse of his naked back
Is driving me insane
Instead of Hail Mary
I'm thinking Kama Sutra positions
Is he flexible enough for all 64?
Enough of this mess
I know what I'm going to do
Get out this car
Walk up to the door

knock ***knock

Not like he hasn't gotten it before

> *Would you be mine?*
> *Could you be mine?*
> *Won't you be my neighbor?*

Translations

Pardon me....
Can you repeat that
I think you are speaking English
Mixed with a dialect that is foreign
...I believe in the vernacular it is called Love and Commitment

This confusion is more than interplanetary translation error
Those that came before you made masterfully constructed language barriers
Blending words with hormones, making a mockery of emotion
Encasing my heart in a way that makes your words alien
My ears seemingly engaged
Mind busy searching for the actual meaning
To what you are saying

Forgive me for asking you to repeat yourself
I think you are speaking English
I want to make sure I am hearing your right

The mother tongue often slanderized
Recognition that words mixed with actions
Folded with emotion
Expressing intention
This romance language
The semantic of it seems Etruscan
Like thinking I can send love over the wall via
Passenger pigeon
Both extinct

I feel I have been abducted and dropped here
Accustomed to being on shaky ground
Forgive me if I appear to still be tripping
This landscape is new to me

Maybe if you wrote it down
I'd understand it better
Are there Dead Sea Scrolls or Rosetta Stones
Or maybe a professional interpreter
As we try to decipher an ancient slang—
That commitment you keep talking

Sorry can you say that once again
I need you to slow it down this time

Which dialect of the five love languages?
do you speak?
Which dual translation book do I need?
Touch to Service
Gifts to Praise
Time to Touch
I'd be a willing student
Reference material acquired
Travel warnings scoured
I'm ready to
Familiarize myself with your customs
Study your history
To you I would be a native
Only if you are doing the same
I want to become fluent in you

That Moment

That moment when making eye contact
Goes from ordinary glimpse to intense glance
Holding hands
Touch foreheads
Engaging energy & brainwaves
Strolls through grass on spring days
Feel like walking in the clouds
Hold onto this …
how we vibe this way
Reflect on these moments
For when THAT MOMENT comes
When simple verbal spat turns nuclear
The thought of touching makes skin crawl
Connection lost
Remember those other moments
Love making under shade trees
Up all night talking
Dreaming we'd rather be
Doing something intimate
Communicating without talking
Creating music out of our heartbeats
We need these moments to stay together
Through the rollercoaster that is a relationship
Let's create thousands of 'those moments'

To the Man at Rite Aid

Who Told His Son, "All You Have to Fear is Satan and If You Want to Know What He Looks Like, He Looks Like Her"

Sir—and I only use "Sir" as a greeting for I am lady—introductions will never be necessary; I do not wish to know your name.

If every woman you encounter is a representation of the Devil l than I have to ask what demons you are harboring in that Pandora's Box that you call a brain. Curiosity did not get the best of me; I did not ask for the key nor demand entry, so please capture and subdue the banshee that just came screaming out of your mouth.

If my refusal to be subjugated to your brand of misogyny makes me the Devil then please dust the soot off my throne next to Lucifer, where I will perch myself royally, holding his hand proudly ruling our kingdom of mindless believers like you,

…those so full of demonic energy that you cannot recognize Aphrodite when she is in your midst.

No, I am nowhere near perfect but I'm fuller of life and love than a body of water about to burst through a dam and prepared to flood the town called Bullshit you have built in your brain leaving you looking for

FEMA:
Fucking
Emotional
Man
Assistance
Your paperwork will be lost, discarded and never to be processed for payment.

You do not deserve the remuneration the bounty of love, caring, affection and sex a good woman provides to those that understand their full value. Understand that any amount of trouble and effort to keep them happy is more than worth it. As Athena dressed in all black we would go to war
with you
for you
you barely need to ask us too….

However, you chose to see women as the ultimate enemy whether or not you know us.

Sir, I noticed you could not look me in the eye when you realized I had heard you, which is why you turned to stone when I rotated around to confront you and as I didn't wish to spend the weekend in Baltimore City's secure bed and breakfast I left with you with a just a withering glance. You're probably still standing there with a look that is dazed and confused.

Our divinity will not stand to be put under attack daily having it stripped away no matter what we are wearing. I could have been in a burqa or nuns habit the goddess in me would still not be safe from men that view women as property, and yes it was Halloween but, Sir, I'm here in a business suit. Your statement tells me that if I were in jeans and a t-shirt I'd still be disrespected as if I were in here dressed as a prostitute.

As you stand there calling all women Satan, would you have said that if your mother was standing next to you? If our man, best friend, brother, a man who was just taller than you were in the room would you have subjected me and the other woman in aisle between the discounted Halloween candy and Christmas ornaments to your crap you spewed? What does that make you since you since you must have entered Satan's inner sanctum at least once for you created a son? So I ask, as you have taken on the responsibility for the raising and educating of the next generation, why do you insist on procreating hate and chauvinism?

Sir, until you do right by me (and all women), everything you even think about gonna fail!

Cracked

Black don't crack

Supposed to be a complement to black women
How we don't show our age

Black is not allowed to crack

Constantly being told if you are going through hell keep going
But never let them see you sweat
We get plastered
We fix our faces
Pile on a bunch of make up
Cover the cracks in the foundation
All the while inside slowly dying
Looking FLAWLESS
Maintaining our "strong black woman"
Expected by society

So the Black won't crack

We will swallow everything
Stuffing issues on top of other people's crap on top of hurt
Never tell anyone exactly how you are feeling
Answer every "how are you"
With "I'm ok"
While the world is crumbling
Instead of asking for help
Dash to dark corners to shed a few tears
That's the first way the mess tries to leak out
The insanity is trying to escape asylum through the cells
The pains in odd places begin
All the doctors have no explanations
Just an anti-inflammatory
And commercials
Depression hurts
Waking up in the morning entails 2 thoughts
DAMN I guess it's a blessing I'm still breathing
Thoughts drift to suicide
Not really wanting to die
Just wanting the pain to stop

Depression kills
Depression is killing families
Depression is killing us
Yet we do whatever we deem necessary to
Maintain the monument's facade
Looking so pretty

But black cannot crack

So we won't tell anybody
Your friends will watch you have a mental break down
Clueless as what to do
Tell you just push the issue aside
Others say just pray
What someone needs to say
Go find a professional's couch on which to lay
God created counselors and therapy
Start talking the confusion out
Soak up a few boxes of tissues
Get to the heart of the issues
Start feeling better
Add the little pills if necessary
They will suppress the blues
Help adjust the view a little
They suppress your appetite
Any more questions about how I lost the weight
Something my doctor did desire
Not exactly what the doctor prescribed
Yes, my black did crack
The walls fell
I have swept away the debris
Started rebuilding
Gave myself permission to say
NO I'm not OK
Until the day I will be again

Split Second

There is a split second of bliss
That exist only once in every relationship
between the end of the first date
And the start of the second
Every nanosecond of this time must be savored
Like grandma's fried chicken after church on Sunday
It's all anticipation
Excitement

We haven't fucked it up yet
All the possibilities
From one night stand to a couple of forevers exist

We are still perfect on our best behavior
Afraid of making that mistake
That will dispel the magic

Wanting to write one of those silly notes
Do you like me? Check yes or no

During this time, all the sappy stuff they say in love songs make sense
Makes me want to write one of those perfect love poems
I want to save this moment
Relive each stolen glance
Remember that for an instant
There was room to dream

Wonder what that first kiss will taste like
Will laying in his arms feel like home
The rest of the thoughts have me
Blushing, staring into my phone so hard
Other people notice
This is a high that has you wanting to rush in
Skip difficult questions
Fill in the answers later
Enjoy the happy
Forget that the test was set up
That way for a reason
I've failed these tests before

The fear is paralyzing
Keeping you trapped in a self-made prison of disbelief
that this is something that could really be
Maybe I should leave it alone
Looking in the mirror

I see that God with a baby's body over my shoulder
 arm cocked back ready to release the bow...

Hey, Cupid, bring that in a little,
Not ready for that
Not sure if I want that arrow to miss or connect
I want to enjoy each and every one of these nanoseconds

Poison

She was pure
Spirit as pristine as ground after a freshly fallen snow
She came from a good home
Her parents who played their roles
Mama taught her how to be a lady
Daddy showed his princess how one was to be treated
They made sure she knew how to use her manners and brains
To get she wanted and needed
She was overprotected thus
Easily deceived thought had the world on a string
And that she was ready for anything

Then she met him …
The physical embodiment of her dreams
Smart confident with light eyes and innocent smile
She so caught up in the fairy tales in her mind
She thought the rhythm in his walk
Was a love song when really it was to the beat of atomic dog
No matter how many times she saw sign
She still believed all his lies
As they all ended with I love you princess
He was showering all his insecurities onto her
Told her that her beautiful was cursed
Had her believing her significance
Was directly related to her oral skills
And 180 days he stripped off her self-worth
And it wasn't until the fifth woman came to her door screaming
Why was SHE fucking with "her man?"
That she finally found
The strength to cut him loose
Due to how the ending came
She was left with venom
Unfinished business
Instead of using the antidote that is time to clear them through
She took her disillusioned mind back into the dating pool
And took her issues out on him
He was a good guy
His mind was as open as the night sky
The twinkling behind his eyes were the dreams

He was making into his reality
He thought she was perfect
But he forgot the lesson
From that old song
"Never trust a big butt and a smile"
He knew she was emotional, broken and insecure
He thought he could fix it
The strength of his love would make her whole again
He would give her everything
Make her his queen
No matter how many times she lashed out
He believed eventually it would change
Ultimately, she would appreciate him
Reciprocate his affection
But her soul was so corrupted
That she could not see the king she had
She ran after the bad boys because drama was more exciting
Until she found out she was with child
That she decided to settle down
He was more than happy
Because she told him he is gonna be a daddy
It wasn't until the results of the DNA
That he found out how badly he had played

He finally sent her on her way
Now more bitter than baker's chocolate
Living with her rained in trust issues
Stuck in that poisonous cesspool
That he couldn't smell the sweetness of the roses
he was giving to the new girl
Her spirit is beautiful
Not as naïve as the rest but still unaware
That she sits in the eye of a cyclone of
Relationship bullshit
That is three relationships old
She wants to give him her love and her soul
But I am praying that she is able to get away
Break the cycle, find freedom
Before she becomes more poison

A Little Bit…

Hi my name is Sherri
I'm a bitter woman in recovery
Disregard how I caught it
Forget how I display it
Let's rejoice for a moment
 I've found the cure for it
Men I need your help
The remedy
And yes there IS a remedy
Must be given in many small doses DAILY
Assist me in forgiving the ones that hurt me
To look forward to the ones that help me
Jog my memory that all men are not hurtful
I'm asking for LITTLE Things
I just want…
I just need
To fall in love with men every day
Just a little bit
If you please
Wear clothes that fit
Belt above the hips
Upturn your lips
Smell good for extra credit
I need never to know your name
Never see you again…
I'll be in love for two seconds baby
Look for a door to hold
Offer to carry that heavy load
Give up your seats on public transportation
Put yourself in a little danger
Stop metro train doors from closing
So the elderly lady exits the train at her station
Yes, I know…
You may be met with less "thank you" and more scowls
You may not be put first
But recognize that another woman was a witness
 smiled fell in love with men again
just for a second
Taken back to a time when
Substance was more important than swag
Showing good manners is now called thirst

We forget how rare it is to see a man
Those that put women, children and the elderly FIRST
These small acts of valor should not be rare
Chivalry should not be uncommon…
Be like COMMON the artist, who, during his club performance
Bent down to give
Several 30 second private concerts to women ahead of me
(She was in a wheelchair)
A simple act that cost him NOTHING
But gained the love of at least one woman forever

Gentlemen…
Be a gentle man
I'm a bitter woman in recovery
Smooth the way for the next one to break through
Check in on your friends that are girls
Just say hey is everything ok
It's a tiny expression of their importance to you
Text or email will do
Reminder on our lonely days
We are really not alone out here

Acknowledge the man standing next to me
Though only friend he may be
The respect shown is respect given
You've made it a little easier for the next one to break through
Genuine compliments are accepted graciously
Extra points for creativity
Poets, limit the 'ho' and 'bitch' references …
Please speak lovingly of your lady…of all ladies
At the end of this evening
Take a little responsibility for my safety
Walk me to my car
Walk by my side
Adjust to be curbside
Warm and fuzzies will abound
These small acts
Gentlemanly behavior costs nothing
But go a long way to melting iced hearts.
So I again ask again: Gentleman, be gentle men
Please… Let me fall in love with men every day

JUST a little bit…

Superman

What happens when you learn that superman can't fly?
When we discover that all his great feats
And all his amazing deeds are nothing
More than the delusional dreams
Of a reporter for the Daily Planet?
Is the good feeling he left in his wake
Washed away like sediment in the tide?
Can it be re-deposited somewhere else
As hope since we are living in pessimistic times?
What if Peter Parker took pictures?
That spun into a web of deception
That allowed us to believe
That we can be greater than any of our fears?
Will the foundation crumble
Under the weight of newly discovered perjury?
Or maybe with a little trust and a huge dose of faith
Can it still grow stronger over time?
Should a hero's legacy be diminished because we discovered
that they are more human than they are God?

Maybe when the media stops trying
To shape the opinions of mindless minions
We can stop building up these fragile humans
Be a little more merciful and find a little peace on earth
Yet they are set up on granite pedestals in marble temples
Make them out to be immortal
Only later to bring out the hammers and chisels
To slam them back down to terra firma
And then wonder why we have no hope
Why we have problems trusting
Ponder why the world has no spirit that is loving
When we are told that every hero
Is so flawed and imperfect
And how dare we accept it

...in a time that spirals towards expectations
So unattainable
That everybody is breaking under the pressure
Running to the doctors to get medicated
Because they can no longer get away with faking it

But tomorrow there will be another false idol in the making
Ready to take on the superficial benefits of fame
Lead to think that they are more god than human
But for me I will remember the truth
We are not perfect
We are just individual spirits existing plain
Trying to make it and have something to believe in
So for me
Superman will stay in the sky

Love Letters

When reading, we don't' fall in love with the character's appearance. We fall in love with their words, their thoughts, and their hearts. We fall in love with their soul ~ Anonymous

A few words from you my beloved Adele have again changed the state of my mind. Yes, you can do anything with me and tomorrow should be dead indeed if the gentle sound of your voice, the tender pressure of your lips, do not suffice to recall life to my body. (Doyle, 2008)

Victor Hugo to Adele Foucher (1820)

There was a time when strangers became lovers only through the strength of their words.
Couples pouring every thought, every emotion,
Every ounce of passion on to paper.
They would pledge to each other write every day
Sending their affection not knowing if or when they were going to answer

He might be off exploring the world
fighting the king's war
he wouldn't know
Would she get the letter?
Would she remember him?
Does she still love him?
Yet he'd keep writing
She'd receive his words on paper and read his prose
Never doubt his love for her

My heart overflows with emotion and joy! I do not know what heavenly languor, what infinite pleasure permeates it and burns me up. It as if I had never loved!!!Tell me whence these uncanny disturbances spring, these inexpressible foretastes of delight, these divine tremors of love. Oh! All this can only spring from you, sister, angel, woman Marie! (Lovric, 2002)

Franz Liszt to Marie d'Agoult (1834)

She knew she was adored
Had a love that would last
regardless of distance
circumstance
Until death did they part

writing a love letter is an art
In today's age
Instant contact
Instant response
Instant connections
instant gratification
It's no wonder why some of our relationships
are like instant oatmeal
mushy, tasteless, somewhat satisfying and gone to quickly

When sentiments must be limited to 140 characters
our affections are required to be abbreviated
IYQ = I like you
ILY, ILU = I love you
LYSM = Love you so much
you send your heart out in characters that 'read'
 less than 3
What is the real meaning
when it can be

copy paste sent
copy paste sent
copy paste sent

how do I know that thought,
that message was really meant for me...
will it last after ... a disaster
One dropped phone,
one spill glass of water

I think he said

I looked to the sky to give thanks for you, whisper a soft prayer for you, blew it to you in a kiss

after x number of messages it
automatically deleted
it has to be remembered
how can it be cherished
read later 10, 20, 30 times
held close to the chest
the emotions in email are real
but the letter gives something to feel

without you, dearest I couldn't see or hear or feel or think - or live - I love you so and I'm never in all our lives going to let us be apart another night. (Lowenherz, 2002)

Zelda to F. Scott Fitzgerald 1920

We used to put our most complex feeling
onto paper
Fold it like origami
pass it under the desk in class
praying your intended gets it
before the teacher
we were taking risk
who had the teacher that would find it
read it in front of the class
how embarrassing could that be
But the reward would be worth it

We'd have each other's words
written in our own hand
I could keep his words in a box
have it whenever I wanted to feel that love
for a minute…once again
I could wrap them with a bow
to be found decades later in an attic
bring up smile that only young love can provide
you can read the emotion in the script
Pretty paper, envelopes and stamps are had to come by
Plus, do we have our intendeds mailing address
They have stopped teaching people how to write
letters on a screen have meaning but no feeling
but that is the only way we get our love letters
is electronically…

You have no idea what you are putting me through

I write back:

Yes I do
I want you to know how I feel about you
Have my words to carry with you
Hear my voice when you read them through…
Those messages and this poem is my love letter…to you

Three Generations

Three Generations all called him
Daddy ...
If any of us called he answered
With a wink and a smile
While limited in his formal education
He smarter than most walking the street
He was not afraid of a hard day's work
Keeping his large family fed
Even if it meant navy bean soup
And homemade apple sauce

By no definition of the word was he a large man
But I have yet to meet the man that could fill his shoes
Even though he has been for almost 20 years
Daddy's presence still largely looms
In the life of all of us
His 11 children
His 19 grandchildren
His 8 great grandchildren (at that time 16 now)
Laid on his chest
Listening to the baseball game with him

He was Daddy
Through the good and bad
He was Daddy
That taught his sons how its supposed to be done
He was Daddy
When some thought the role was meaningless
He is Daddy
That still visits us in all our dreams

Even though he has been gone almost 20 years
Somedays I can still smell his cologne
And feel the strength of his hugs
Though the phrase is heading to become antiquated

I am a Daddy's girl
And damn proud to wear that label

Family Tree

"Trees are the earth's endless effort to speak to the listening heaven."
— Rabindranath Tagore, Fireflies

Branches of family TREES
yields leaves that ARE
floating in the wind are still tied to THE
souls to the origins to the EARTH'S
core. The roots are ENDLESS
each person needs to make the EFFORT
research, learn the stories TO
be able to SPEAK
be the storytellers of our history TO
our descendants and their descendants as they are THE
ones who will be LISTENING
retelling the story while we are in HEAVEN.

He Calls Me

He calls me...
baby

He calls me
               beautiful

He calls me he calls me
               My Cherie Amour

Poetry
His pen and pad
be fingers on my skin opening his mind
Releasing his tongue into a freestyle at the base of neck
He calls me

Grounded
Locked into position
Feeling the lightening in our kiss his feet are still earth bound
he finds the surging heavenly
He calls me

Worship
Willing assuming the position 5 times a day
Regardless of the direction my legs may raise he considers me blessing
studied me like religion
He calls me

Fairy
leaving pixie dust on his upper lip vivid colorful other people see it said
there is magic in my pussy with quickly his pride disappears
Because of how badly he wants to be in it
He calls me

Symphony
My frame he his instrument my clit be a woodwind
giving my moans a key and purpose There isn't an Aura he can't replicate
with his fingers strumming the spot the cord that is always G
He calls me

Geometry
deciphered the equation
How my body can be in angles Wrote the proofs
That orgasms can be multiplied Doesn't require advanced mathematics
He calls me

Present
his endowment fitting perfectly
into the box I've graciously provided He holds my legs in a bow
when I unwrap I'm always Overjoyed

He calls me...
baby

He calls me
          beautiful

He calls me he calls me
          My Cherie Amour

As long as I'm screaming his name for the next few hours
I don't care what he's calls me

Works Cited

Doyle, U. (2008). Love Letters of Great Men. New York, NY: St. Martin's Press.

Lovric, M. (2002). The World's Greatest Letters From Ancient Greece to the Twentieth Century. Chicago: Chicago Review Press, Inc.

Lowenherz, D. H. (2002). The 50 Greatest Love Letters of All Time. New York, NY: Random House.